PIANO+VOCAL+GUITAR

THE BEST OF MODERN WORSHIP

WORSHIP TOGETHER®

W9-BSL-785

HERE I AM to WORSHIP

ISBN 0-634-07977-8

HAL•LEONARD®
CORPORATION
7777 W. BLUEMOUND RD. P.O. BOX 13819 MILWAUKEE, WI 53213

Visit Hal Leonard Online at
www.halleonard.com

CONTENTS

ABOVE ALL

Words and Music by PAUL BALOCHE
and LENNY LeBLANC

BETTER IS ONE DAY

Words and Music by
MATT REDMAN

here my heart is sat - is - fied   with - in Your pres -
thing I ask and I would seek: to see Your beau -

- ence.   I sing be - neath the shad - ow of Your
- ty,   to find You in the place Your glo - ry

wings. _____
dwells. _____

Bet - ter is one day in Your courts, bet - ter is

one day in Your house, bet - ter is one day in Your courts than thou - sands

ABOVE ALL ELSE

Words and Music by
VICKY BEECHING

Je - sus,____ my pas - sion in life____ is to know____

BE GLORIFIED

Words and Music by LOUIE GIGLIO
and CHRIS TOMLIN

BE LIFTED UP

Words and Music by
PAUL OAKLEY

BEAUTIFUL ONE

Words and Music by
TIM HUGHES

BEAUTIFUL SAVIOR
(All My Days)

Words and Music by
STUART TOWNEND

44

BLESSED BE YOUR NAME

Words and Music by MATT REDMAN
and BETH REDMAN

Recorded a half step higher.

glo - ri - ous name.

Lead vocal ad lib. to end

Repeat ad lib. and Fade

Optional Ending

FOREVER

Words and Music by
CHRIS TOMLIN

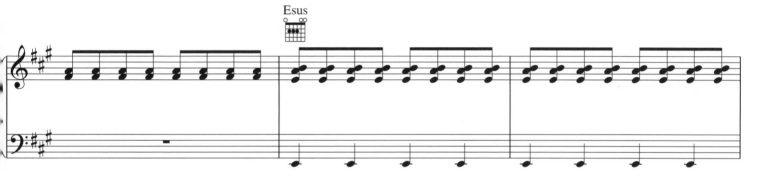

Esus   Dsus2

A

Give   thanks   to   the   Lord, ___   our
With   a   might - y   hand   and   and
From   the   ris   -   ing   to   the

God   and ___   King. ___   His   love   en - dures ___   for - ev -
out - stretched ___ arm, ___   His   love   en - dures ___   for - ev -
set - ting ___   sun, ___   His   love   en - dures ___   for - ev -

D

- er.   For   He   is   good, ___   He   is   a -
- er.   For   the   life ___   that's
- er.   And   by   the   grace   of ___   God ___   we   will

ENOUGH

Words and Music by CHRIS TOMLIN
and LOUIE GIGLIO

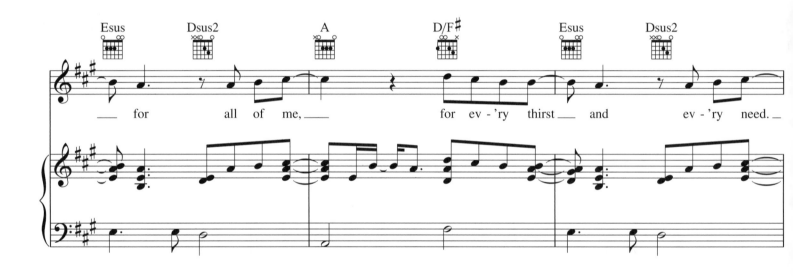

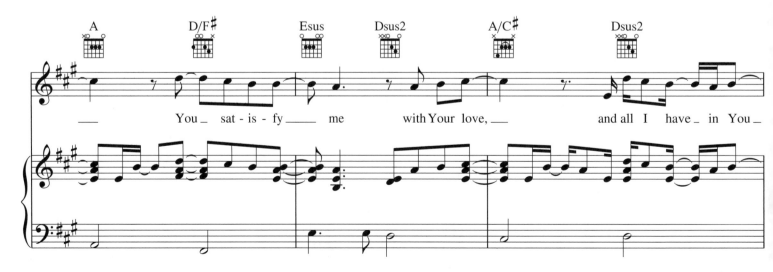

GOD OF WONDERS

Words and Music by MARC BYRD
and STEVE HINDALONG

THE HAPPY SONG

Words and Music by
MARTIN SMITH

Oh,   I   could   sing   un - end - ing
       I   could   dance   a   thou - sand

Solo ends

cel - e - brate, hey, for joy is in ___ this

place. *Vocal 1st time only*
Instrumental solo - ad lib.

Oh, _____ I could sing un -
Solo ends

D.S. al Coda
(Take 3rd & 4th endings)

HERE I AM TO WORSHIP

Words and Music by
TIM HUGHES

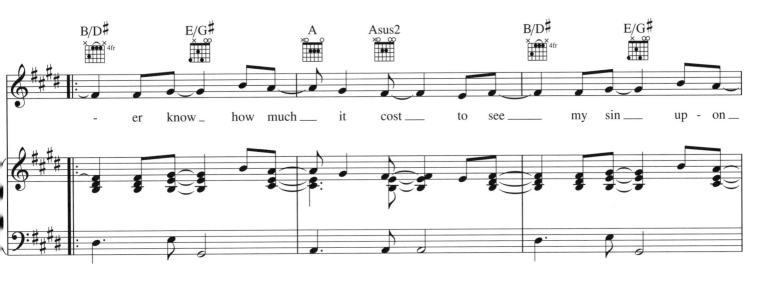

-er know_ how much_ it cost_ to see_ my sin_ up-on_

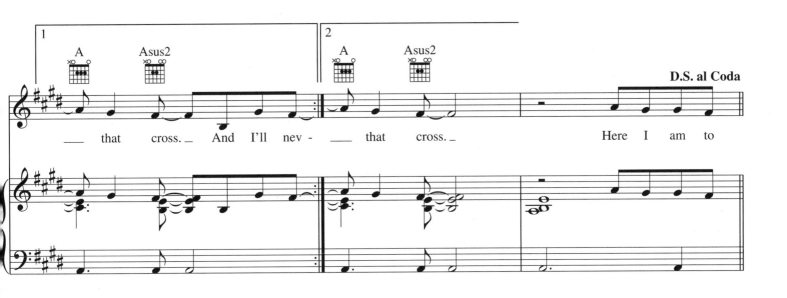

____ that cross.__ And I'll nev- ____ that cross.__ Here I am to

D.S. al Coda

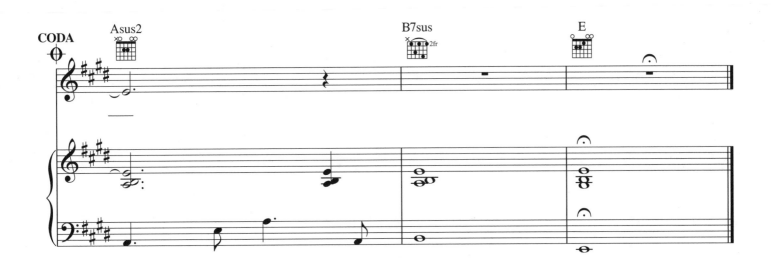

CODA

HOLY IS THE LORD

Words and Music by CHRIS TOMLIN
AND LOUIE GIGLIO

IN CHRIST ALONE

Words and Music by KEITH GETTY
and STUART TOWNEND

30

IT IS YOU

Words and Music by
PETER FURLER

As we lift up our hands, ___ will You meet us here? ___ As we call on Your name, _

___ will You meet us here? ___ We have come to this place ___ to wor - ship You, _

___ God of mer - cy and grace. ___ It is You ___ we a - dore. _

LET EVERYTHING THAT HAS BREATH

Words and Music by
MATT REDMAN

LET MY WORDS BE FEW
(I'll Stand in Awe of You)

Words and Music by MATT REDMAN
and BETH REDMAN

Original key: D♭ major. This edition has been transposed up one half-step to be more playable.

LORD, LET YOUR GLORY FALL

Words and Music by
MATT REDMAN

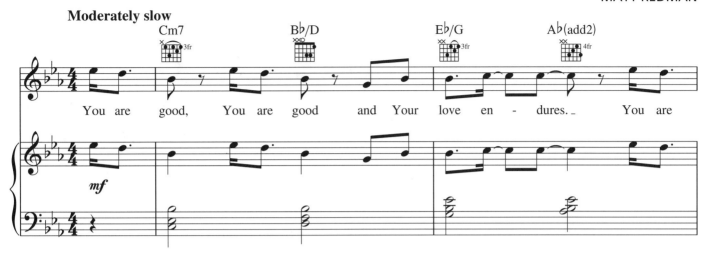

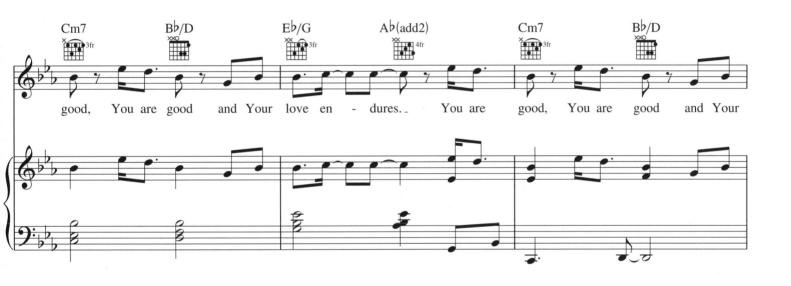

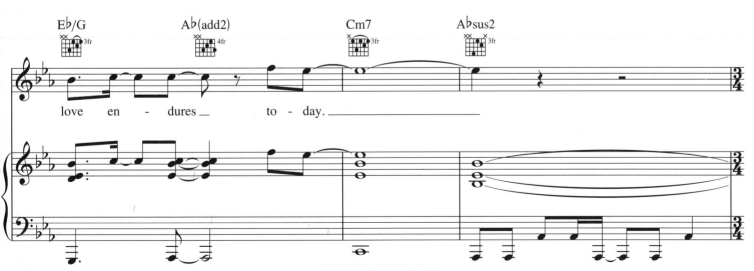

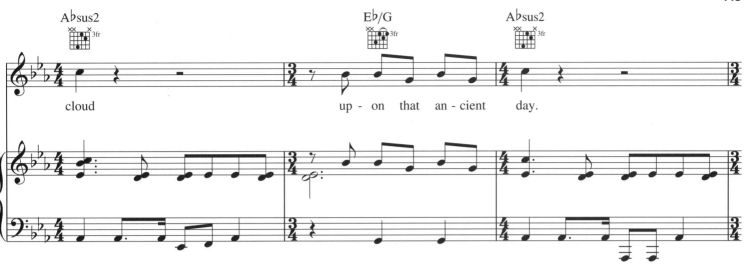

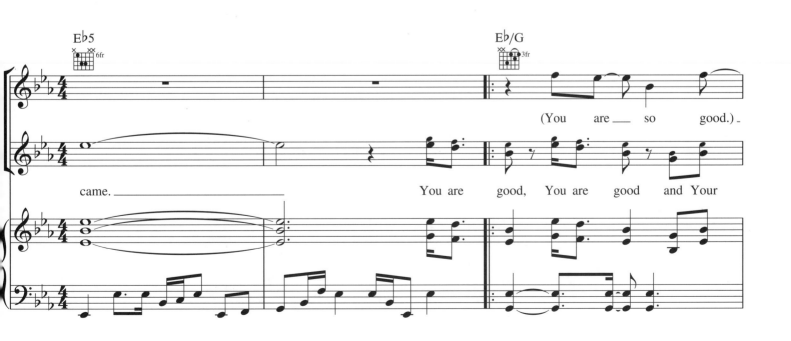

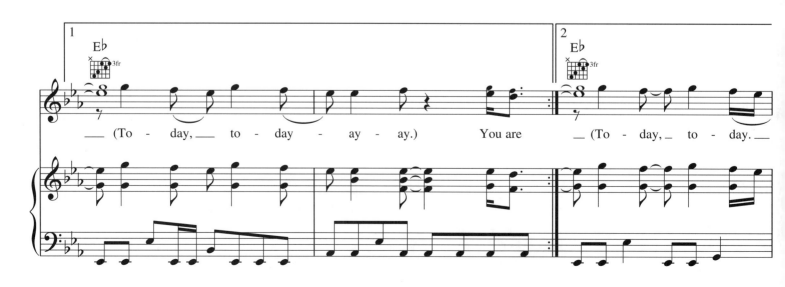

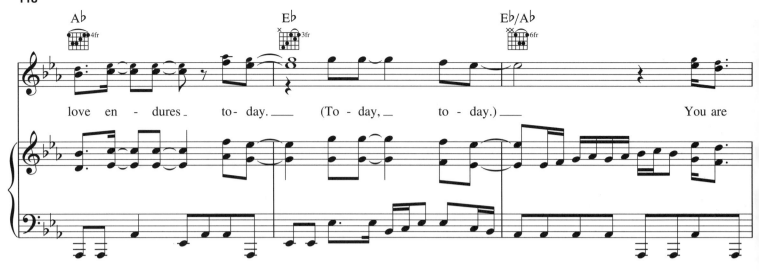

love en- dures to- day. (To- day, to- day.) You are

(You are so good.)

good, You are good and Your love en - dures. You are

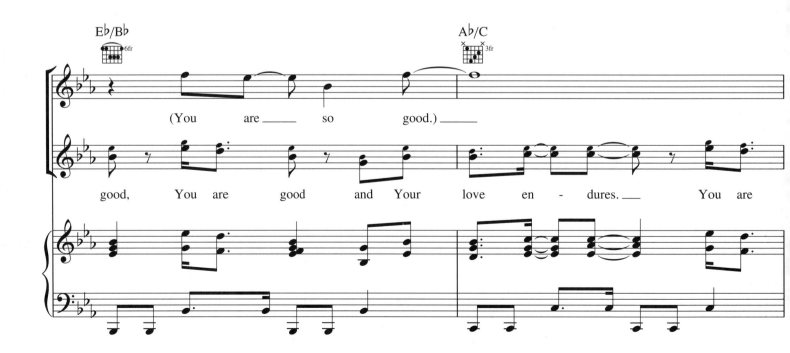

(You are so good.)

good, You are good and Your love en - dures. You are

LORD, REIGN IN ME

Words and Music by
BRENTON BROWN

MAJESTY
(Here I Am)

Words and Music by MARTIN SMITH
and STUART GARRARD

Moderately slow

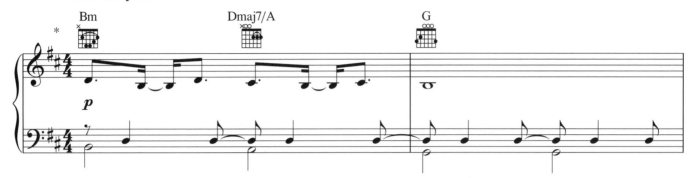

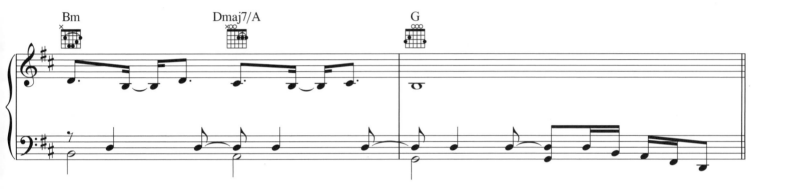

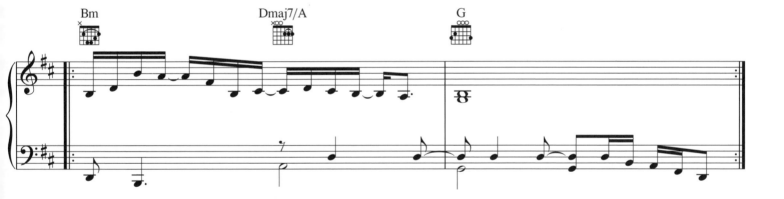

Here   I   am,

Here   I   am,

*Recorded a half step lower.

MY DRINK
(I Remember You)

Words and Music by
CHARLIE HALL

See the blaze that burns _ in me when I _ _ see You and You look at me, _ O Lord. _ On You I med-i-tate, and as _

On You I med-i-tate, and as _____ I think, my soul, it faints _ for You. _

Your bod - y and _ Your blood, _ and I _

O PRAISE HIM
(All This for a King)

Words and Music by
DAVID CROWDER

OUR LOVE IS LOUD

Words and Music by
DAVID CROWDER

UNDIGNIFIED

Words and Music by
MATT REDMAN

Lyrics:

I will dance, I will sing to be mad for my King. Noth-ing, Lord, is hin-der-ing __ this pas-sion in my ___ soul. And I'll be-come e-ven more un-dig-ni-fied than ___ this. Some may say it's fool-ish-ness, but I'll be-come e-ven more un-dig-ni-fied than ___ this.

THE WONDERFUL CROSS

Words and Music by JESSE REEVES,
CHRIS TOMLIN and J.D. WALT

WE FALL DOWN

Words and Music by
CHRIS TOMLIN

YESTERDAY, TODAY AND FOREVER

Words and Music by
VICKY BEECHING

Ev-er-last-ing___ God,___ the years go by, but You're___
Un-cre-at-ed___ One,___ You have no end and no___

___ un-chang-ing. In this fra-gile world,___ You
___ be-gin-ning. Earth-ly pow-ers fade,___ but

Gm7   B♭   B♭6

You are ____ faith - ful and we will trust in ____ You. ____

F/A   B♭sus2   Dm7   Csus

____ We will trust ____ in You. ____

F/A   B♭sus2   Dm7   Csus   F/A   B♭sus2

____ We will trust ___ in You. _____

Dm7   Csus   F/A   B♭sus2

You are a faith - ful _____ God, _____ faith -

YOU ALONE

Words and Music by JACK PARKER
and DAVID CROWDER

(1., 3.) You _____ are the on-ly _____ one I _____ need. _____ I bow
(2., 4.) You _____ have giv-en me _____ more than _____ I _____ could

all of me _____ at Your _____ feet. _____ I
ev-er have _____ want-ed, _____ and I _____ want to

wor-ship _____ You a-lone.
give You my _____ heart and my _____ soul.

YOU ARE MY KING
(Amazing Love)

Words and Music by
BILLY JAMES FOOTE

Worshipfully

I'm for-giv - en _____ be - cause You were _ for-sak - en.

I'm ac - cept - ed; You were _ con - demned. _ I'm a - live _ and well; _ Your

Spir - it is _ with-in _ me be - cause You died _ and rose _ a - gain. _